Coloring in America

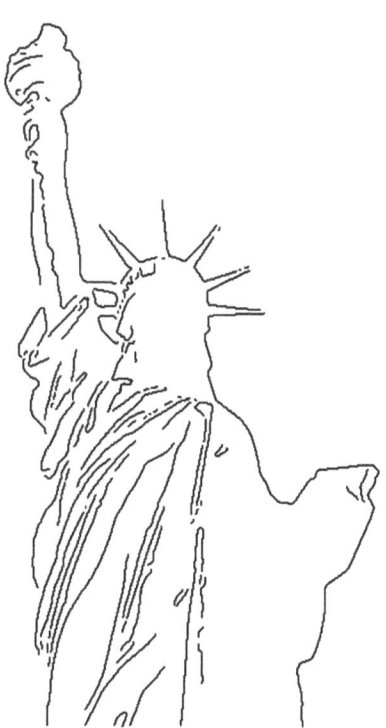

Chloe Metcalfe

Coloring in America

ISBN-13: 978-1534779235

ISBN-10: 153477923X

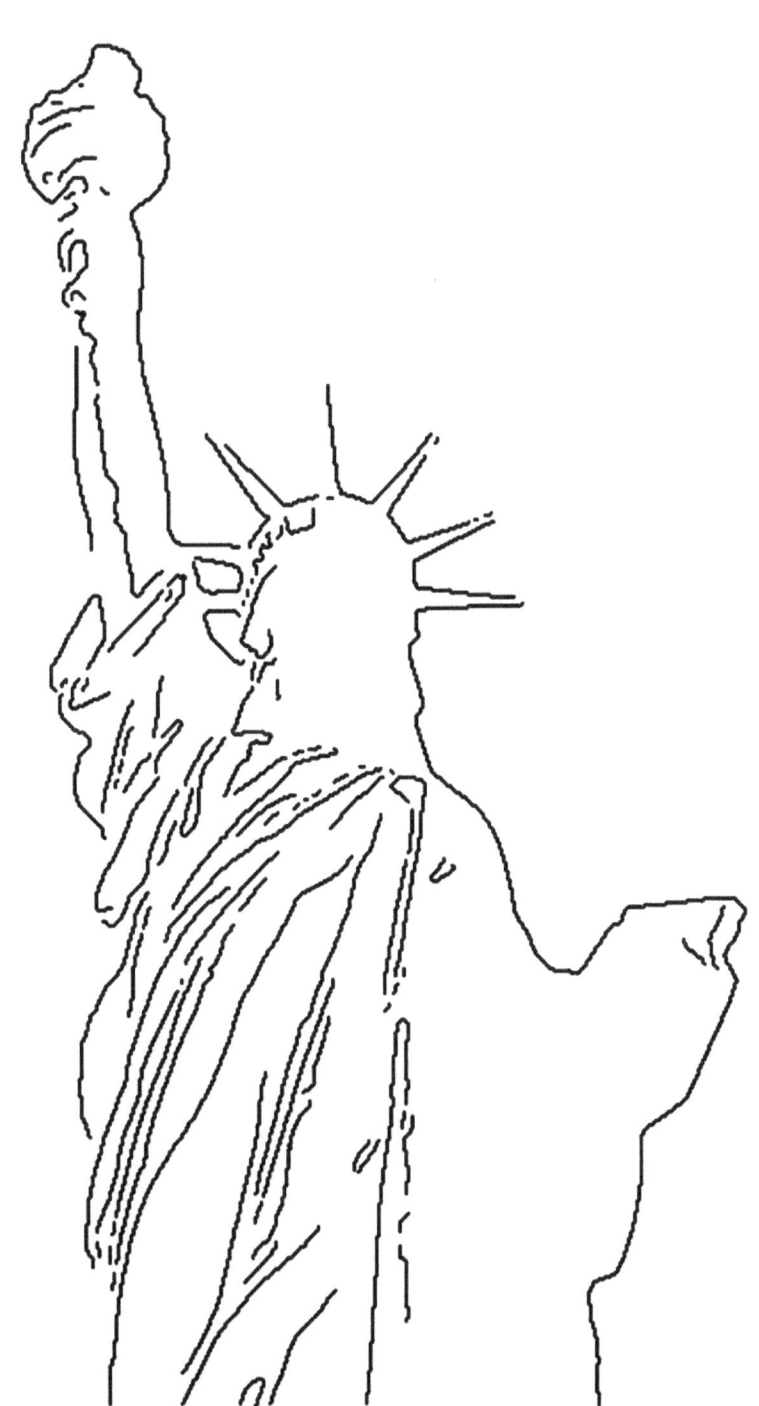

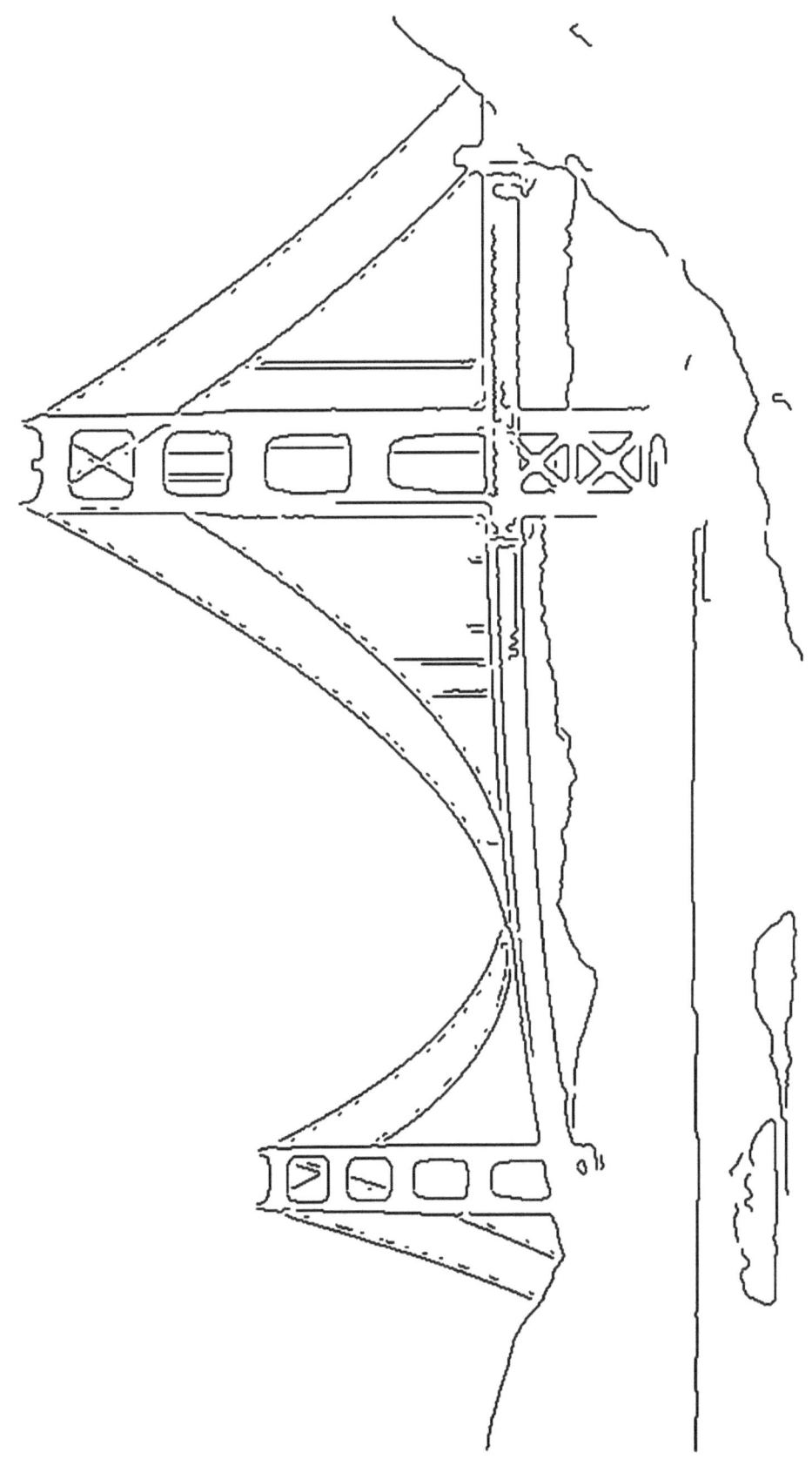

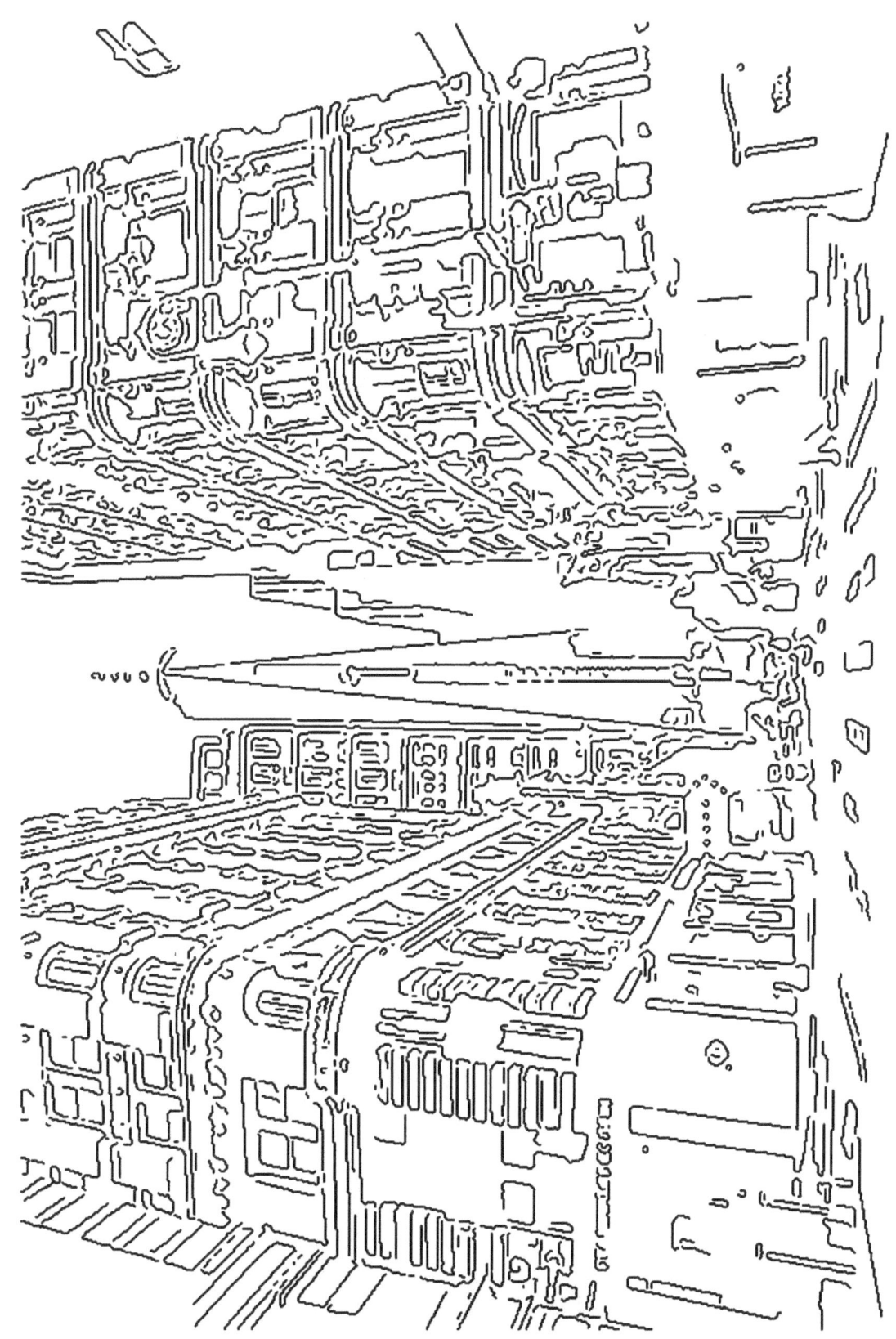

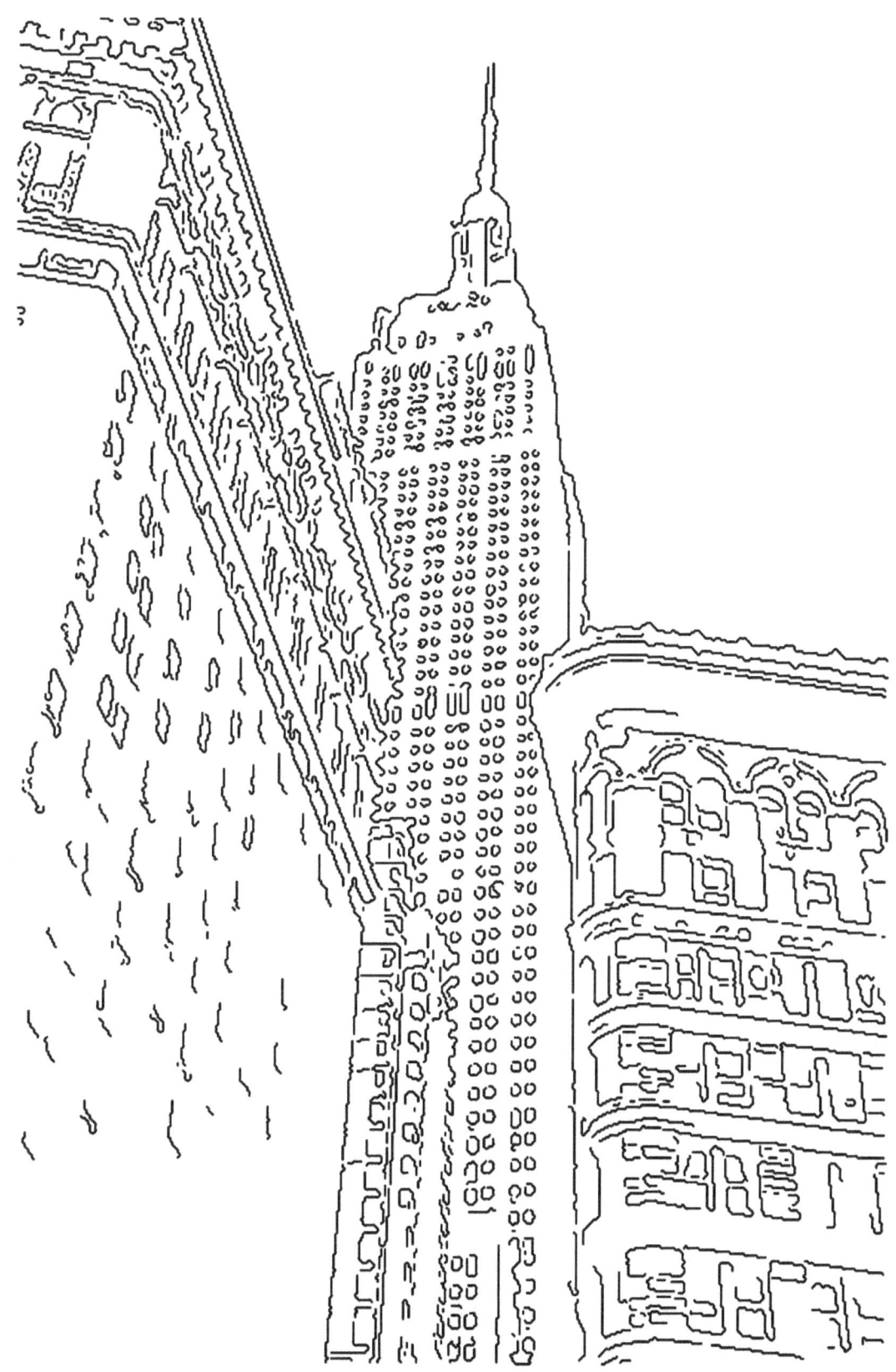

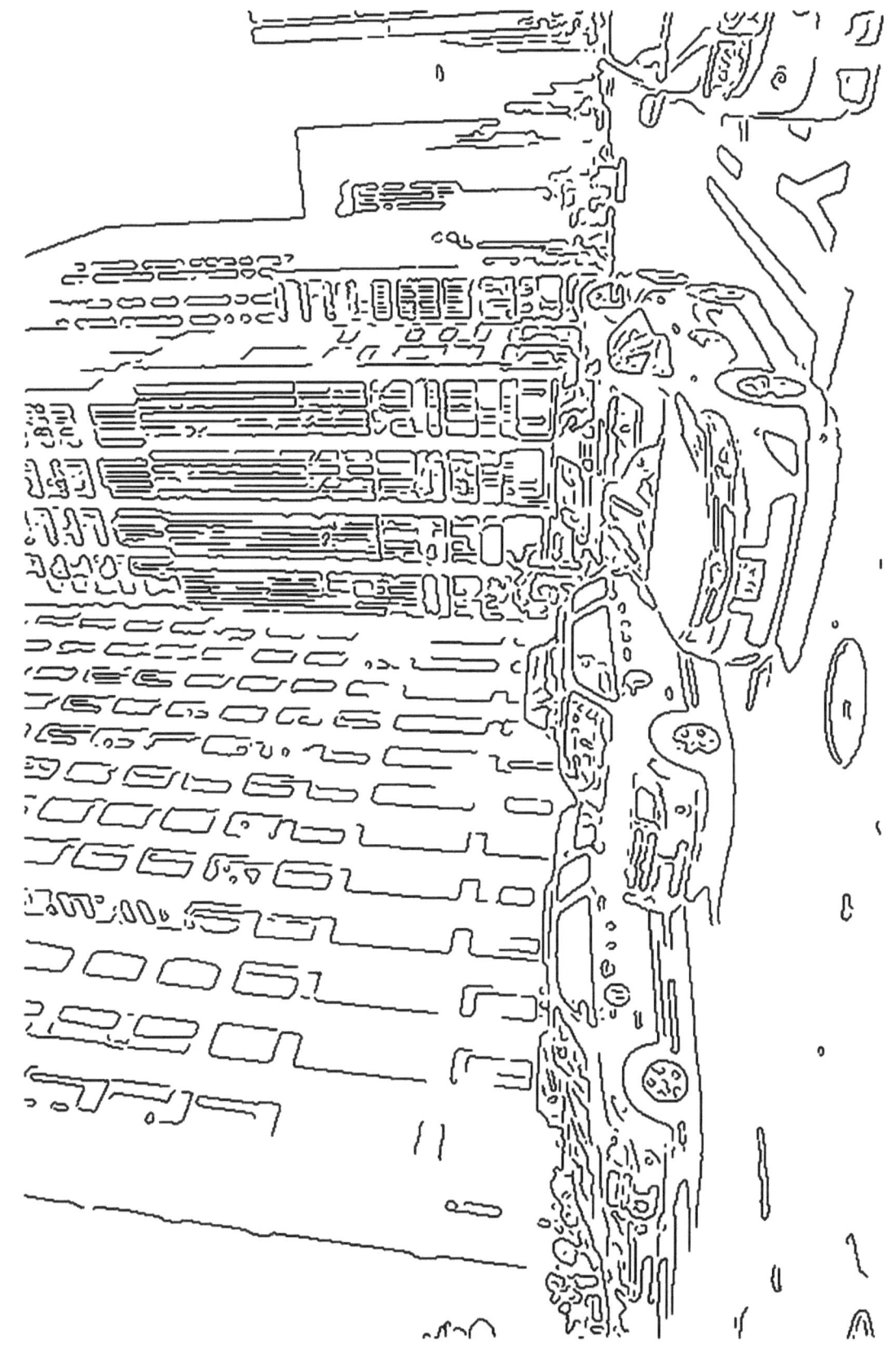

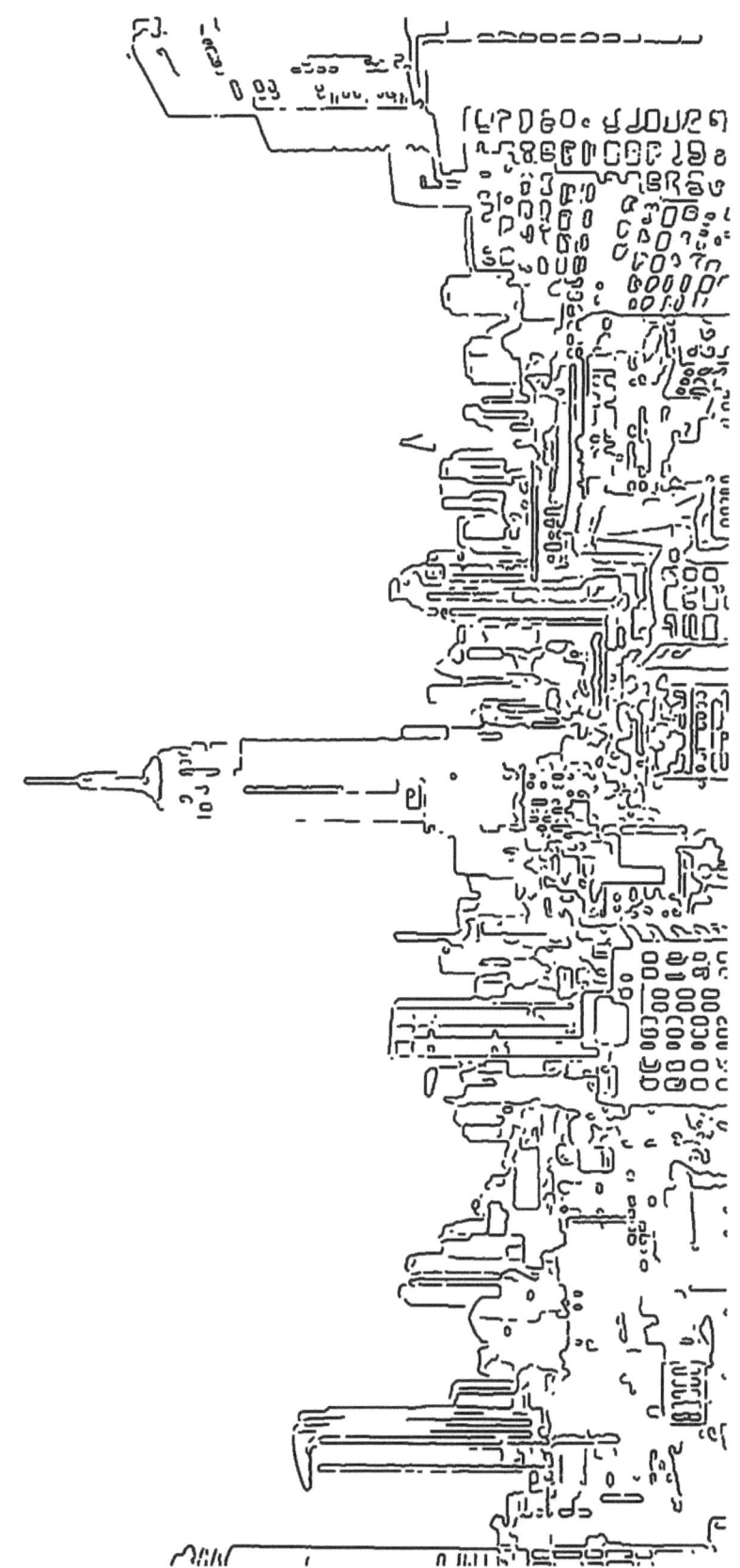

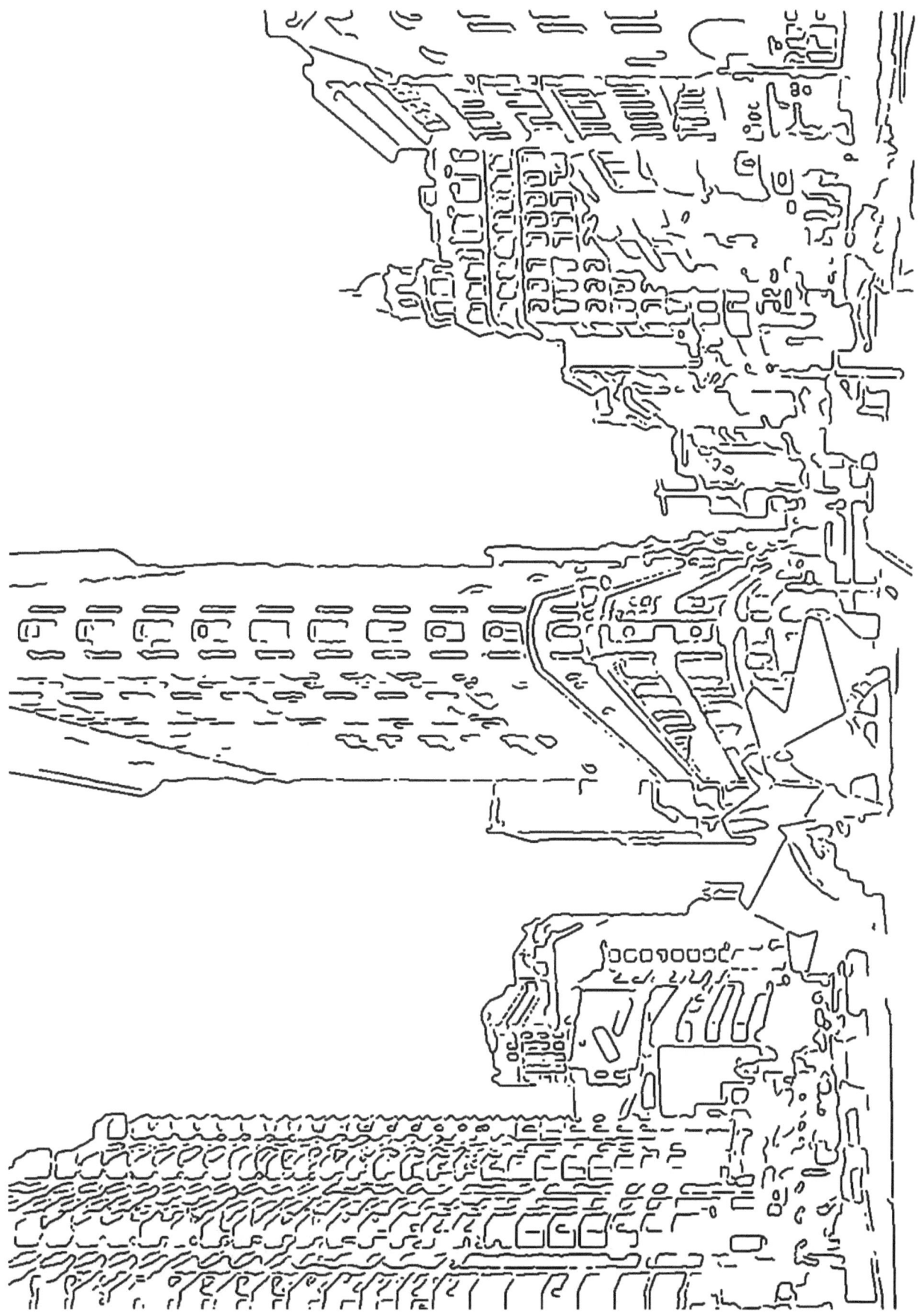

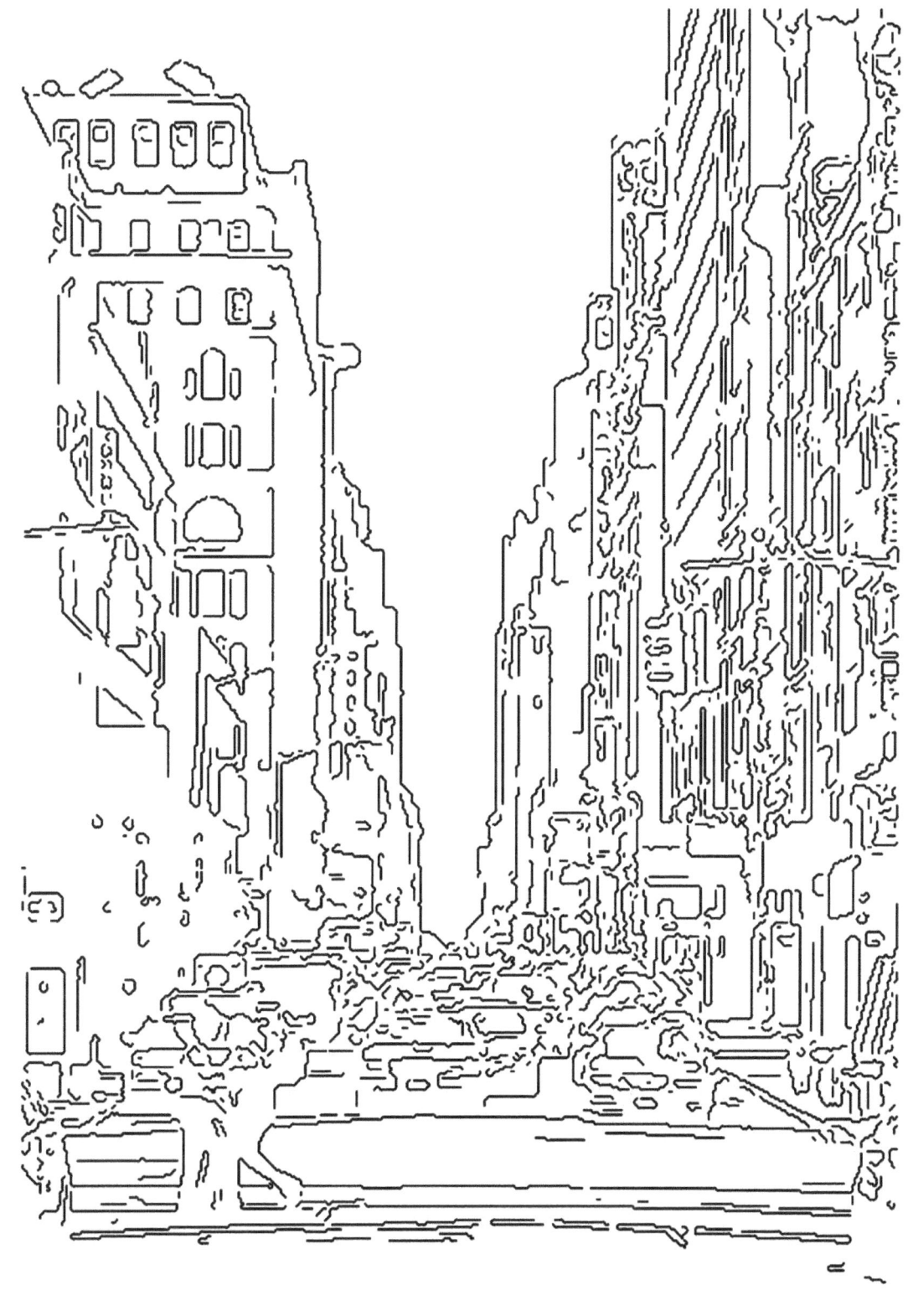

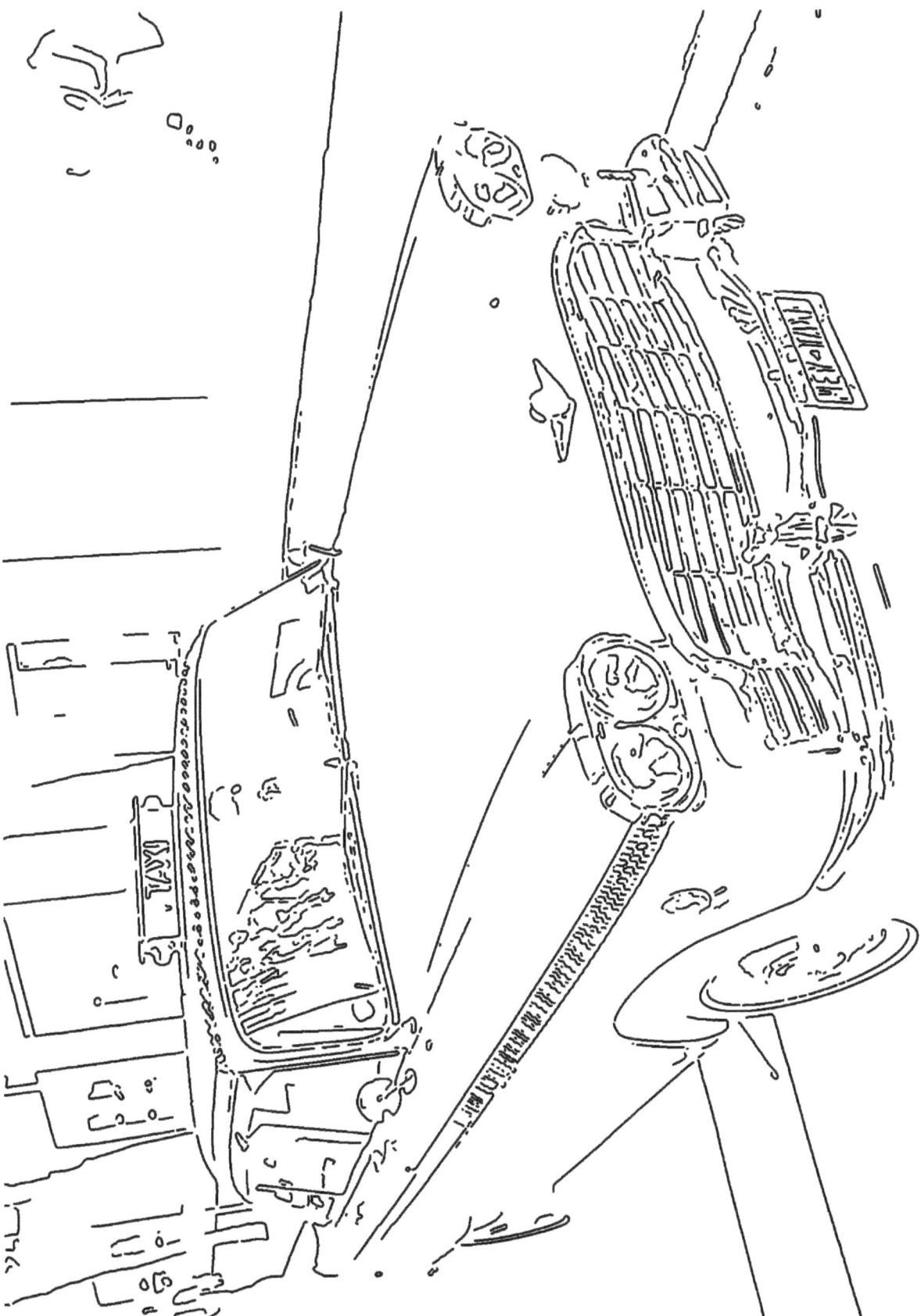

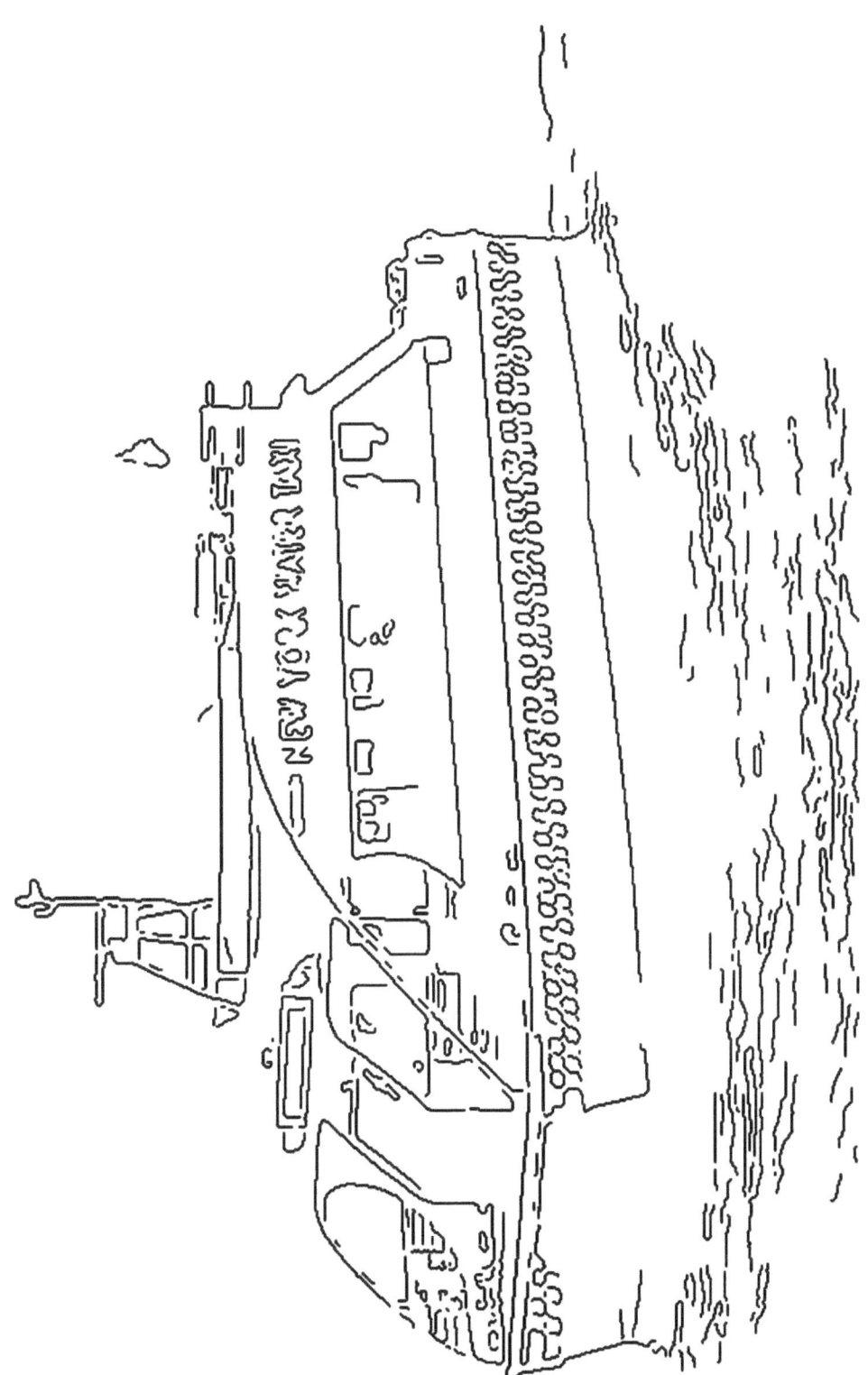

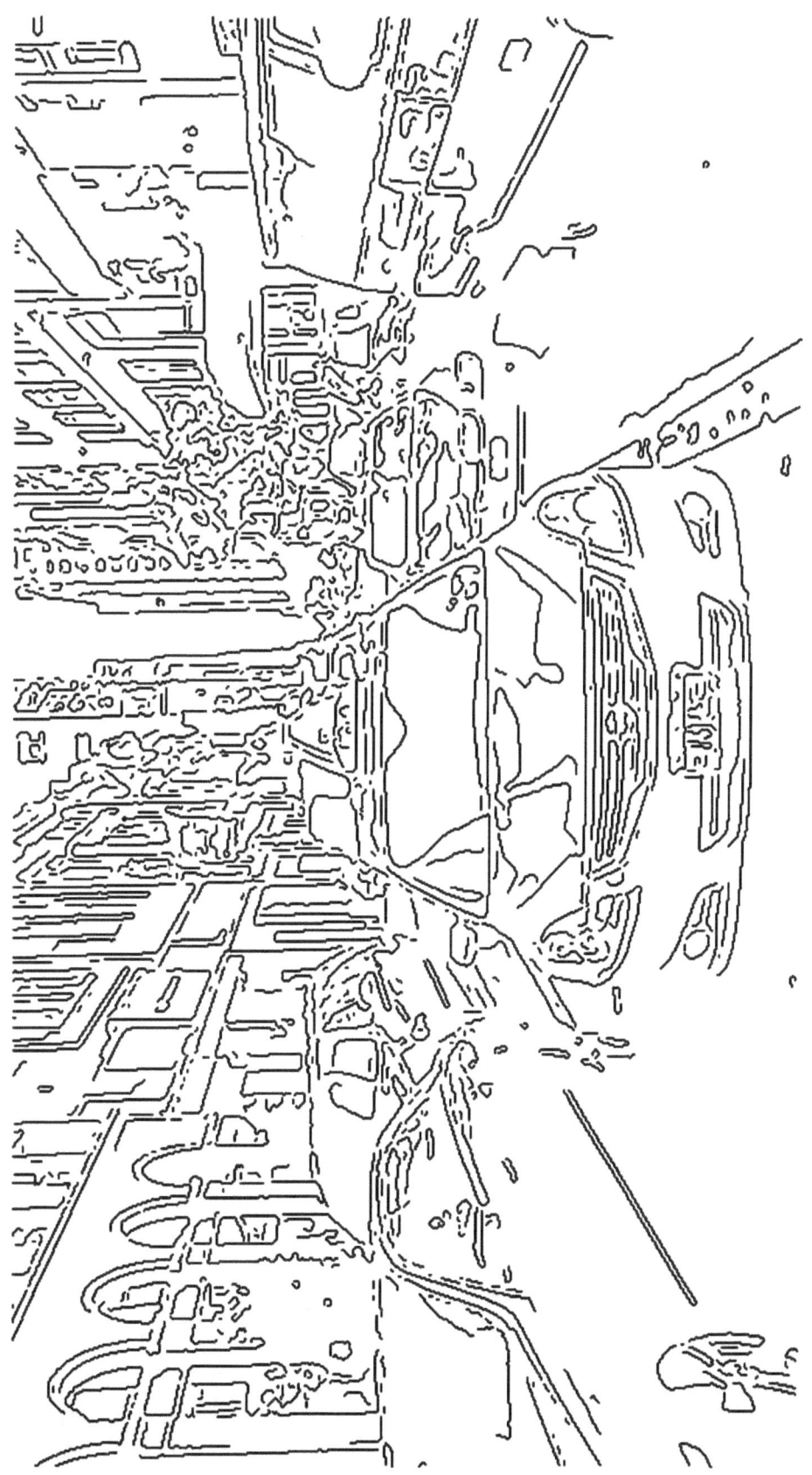

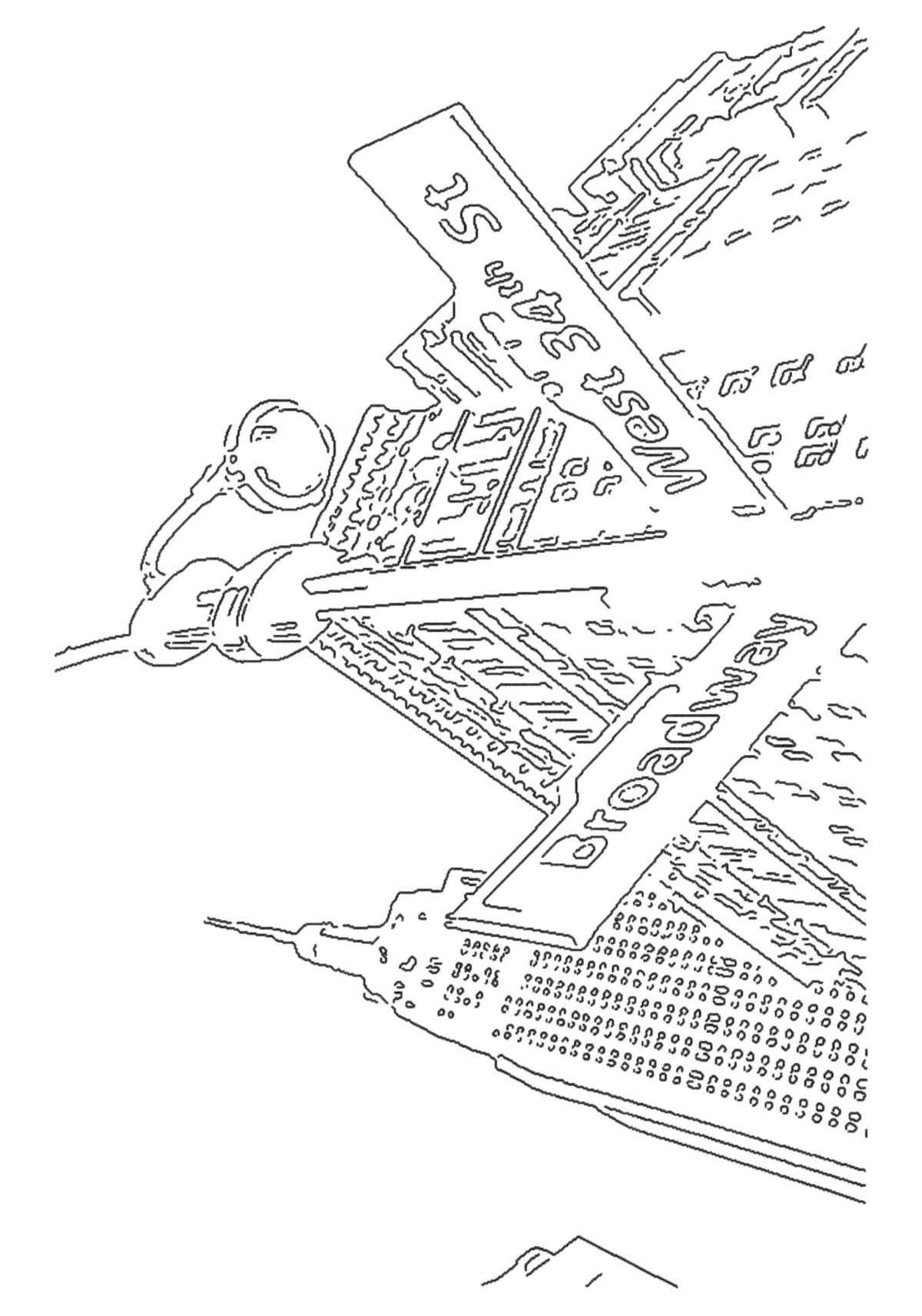

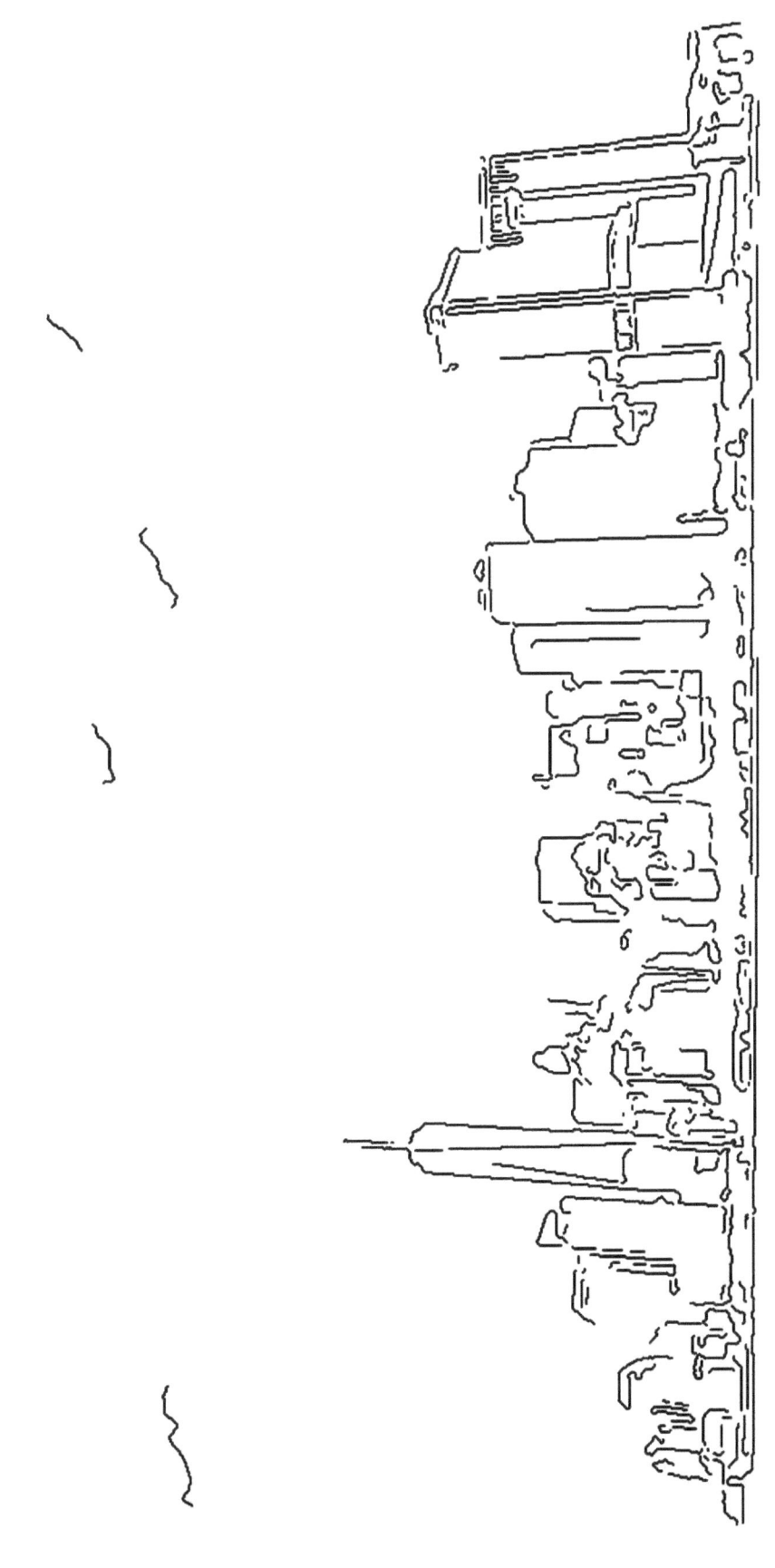

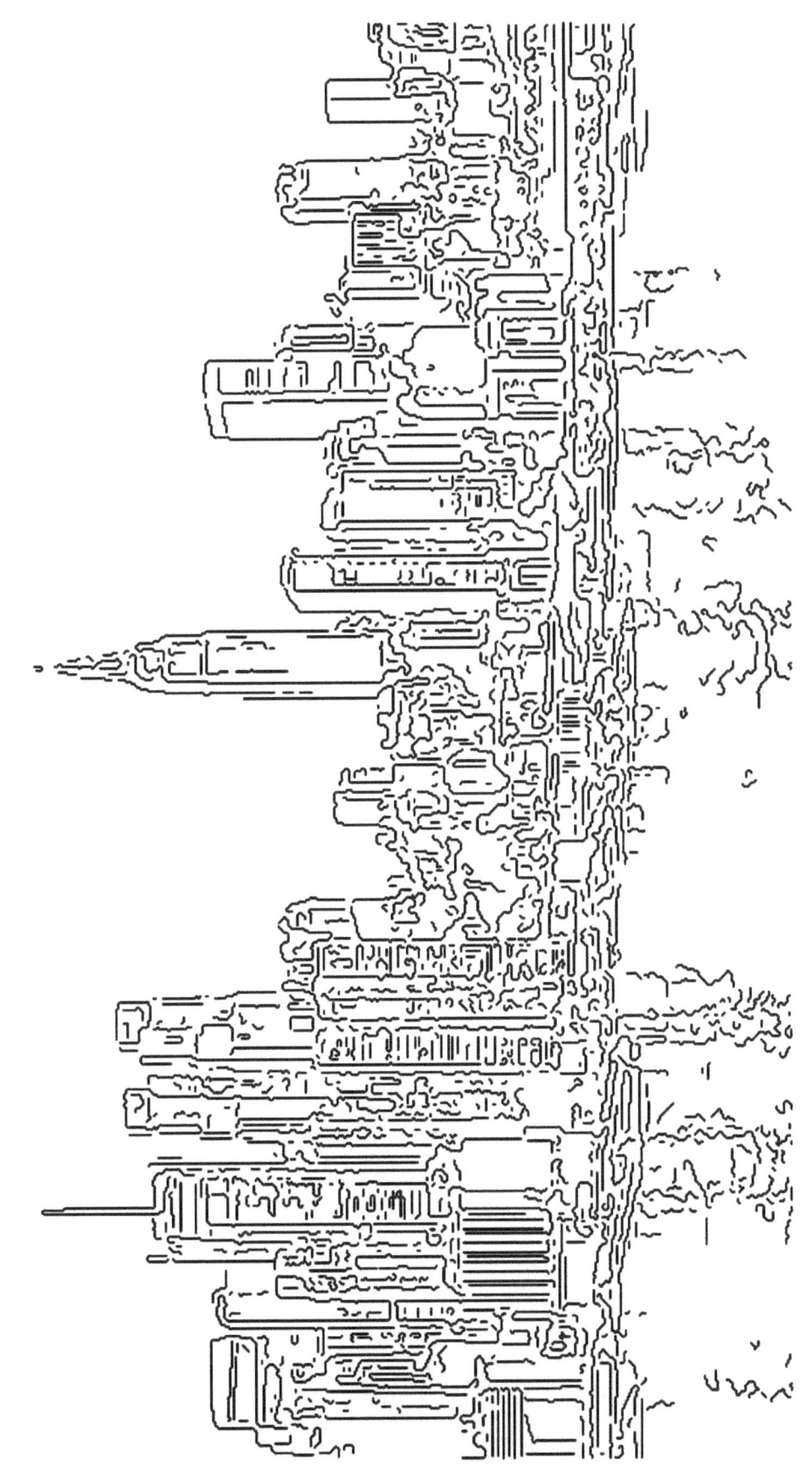

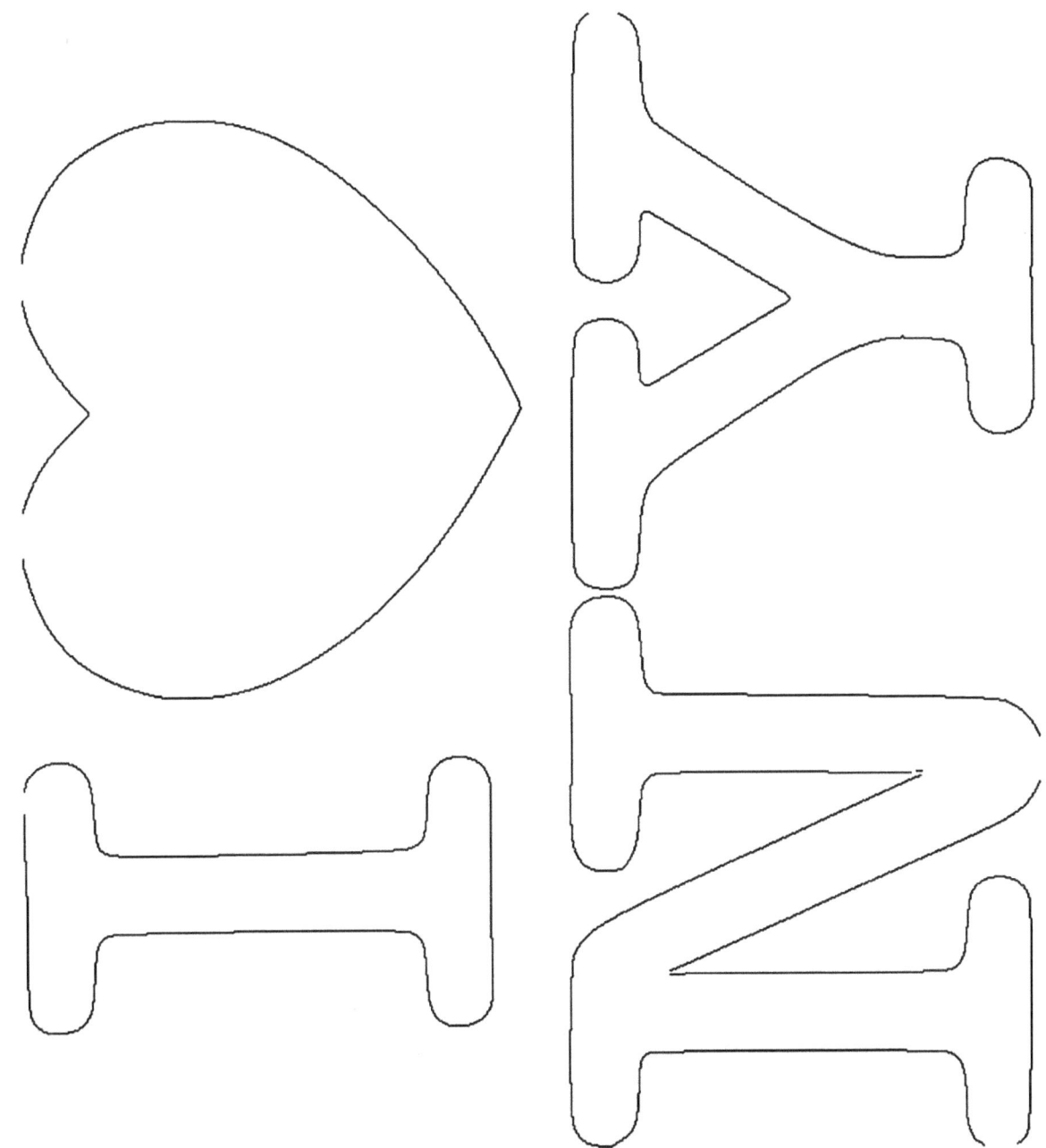

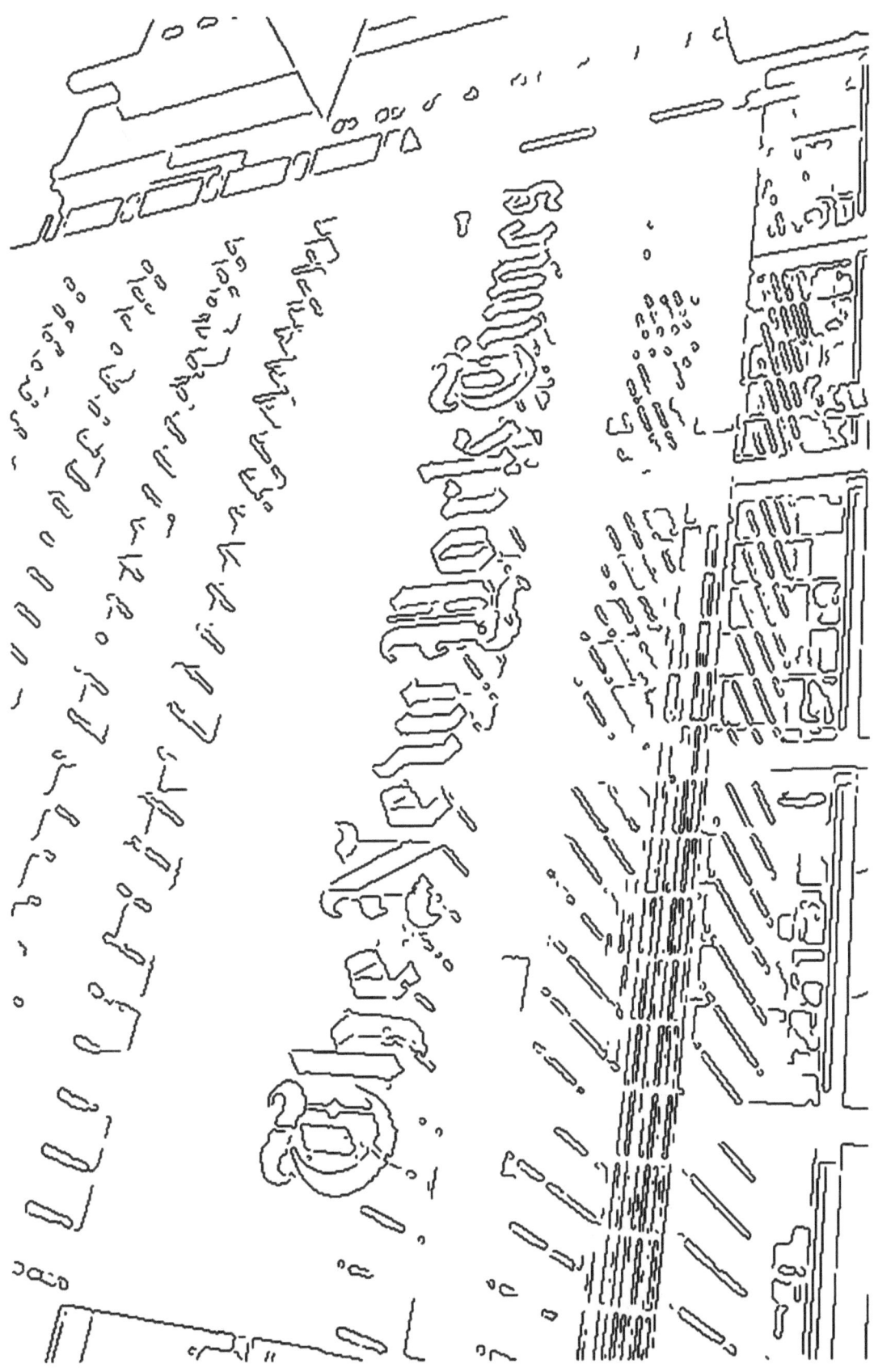

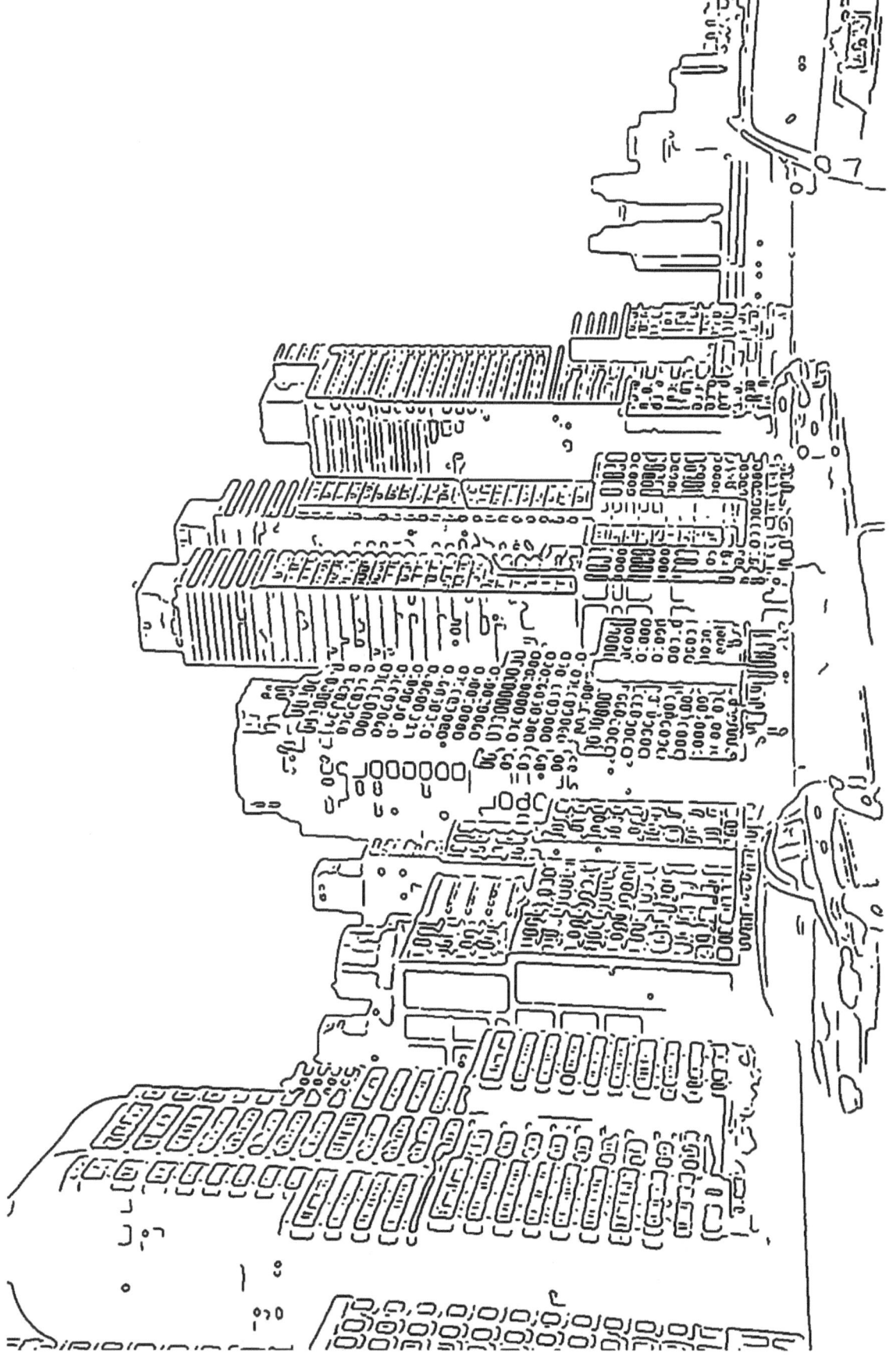

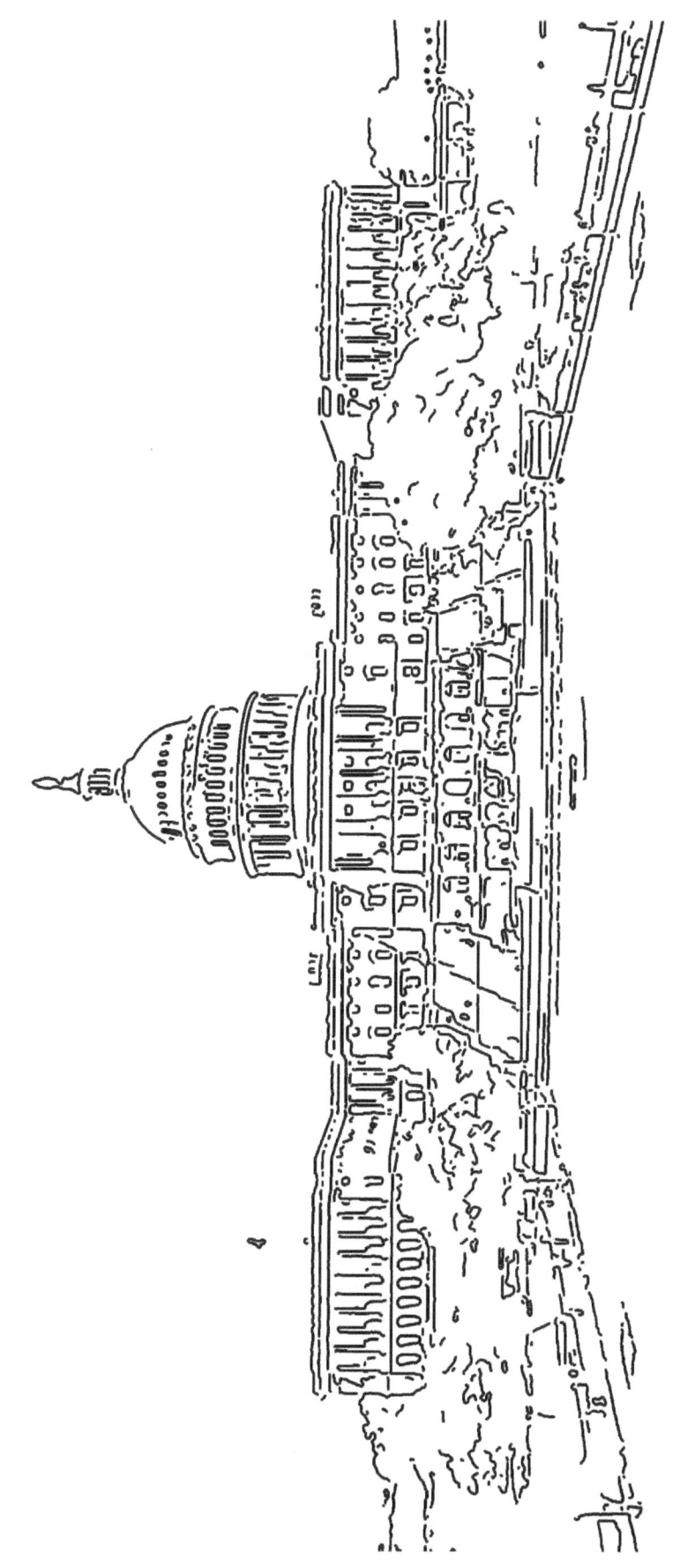

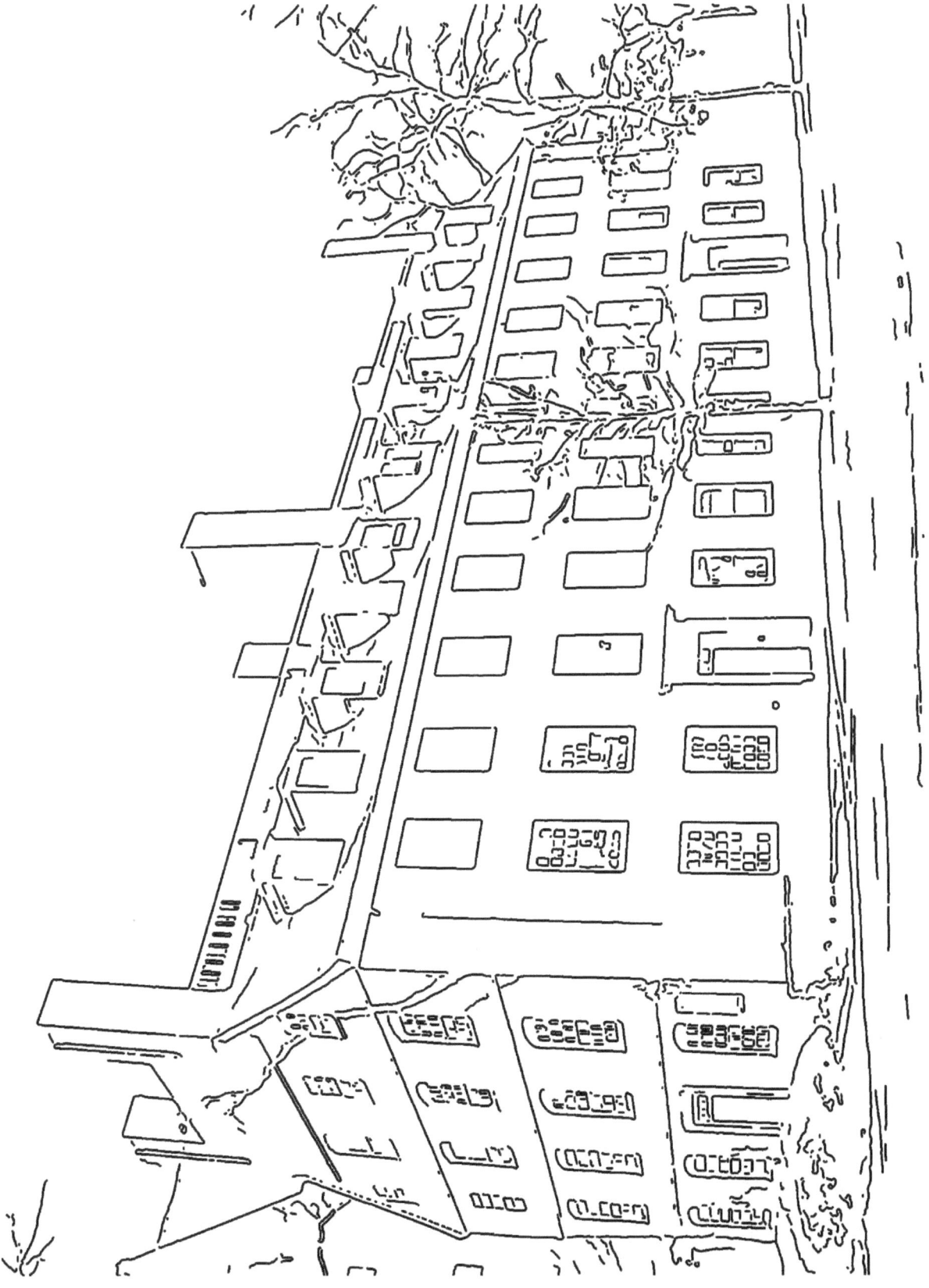

.

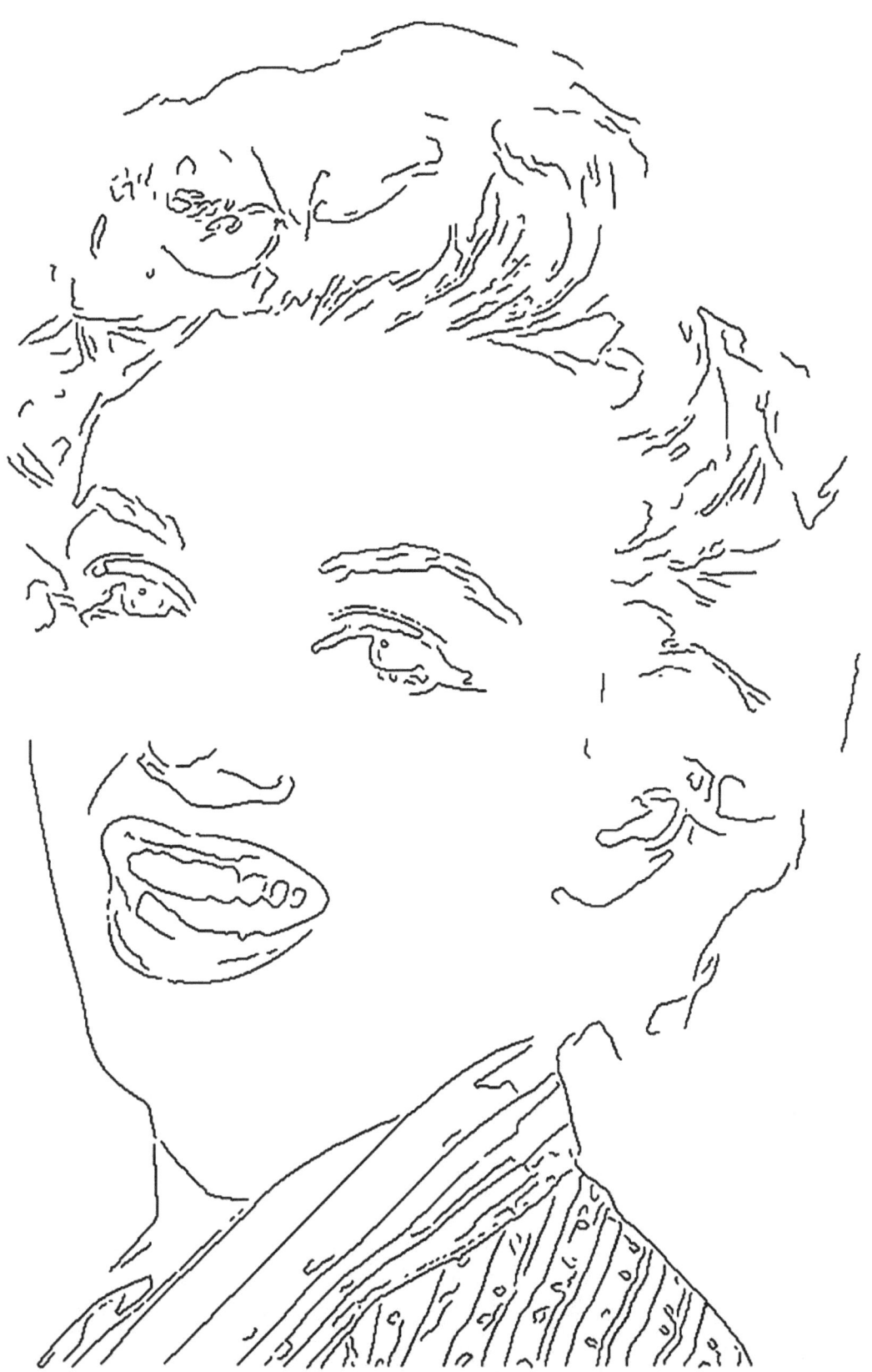

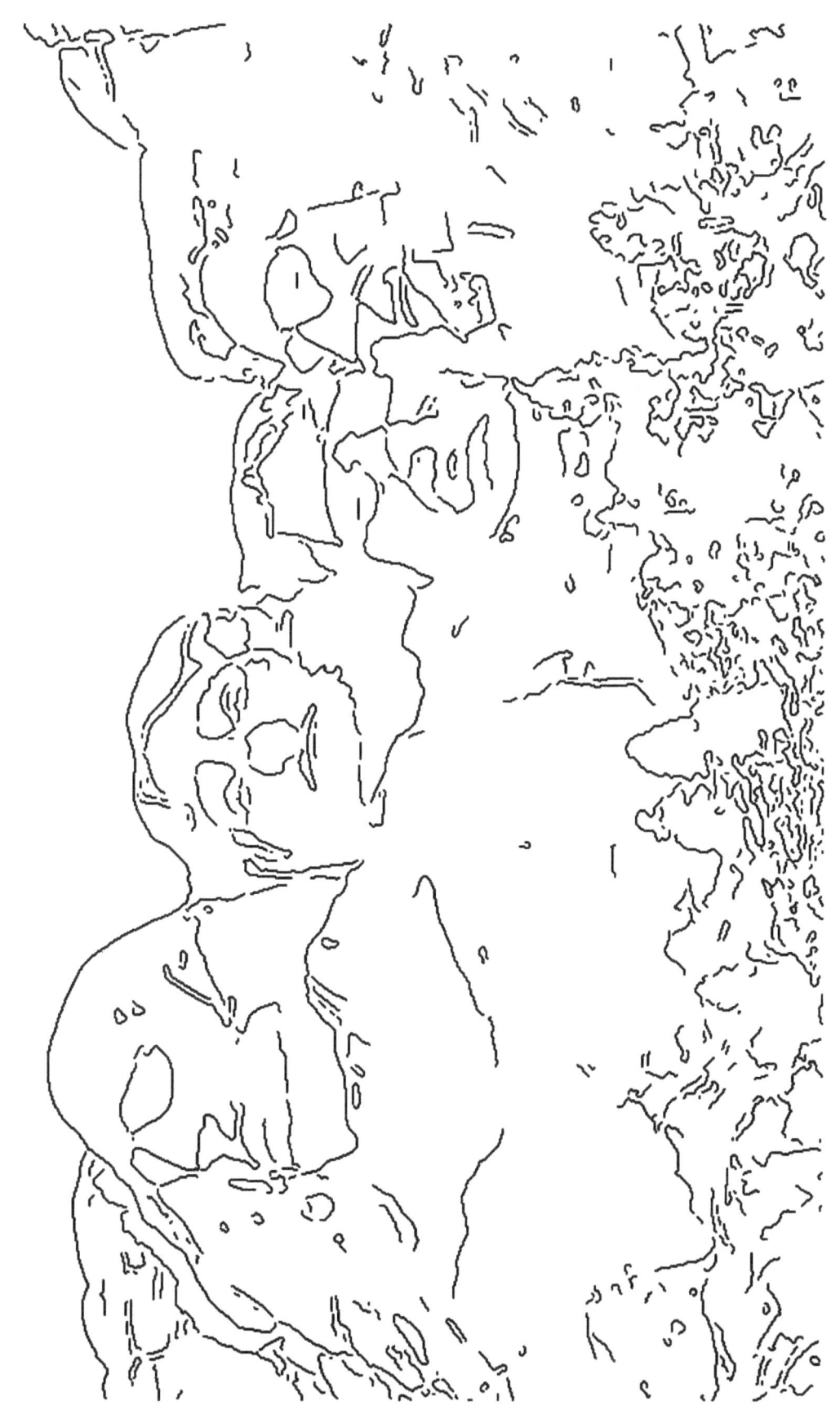

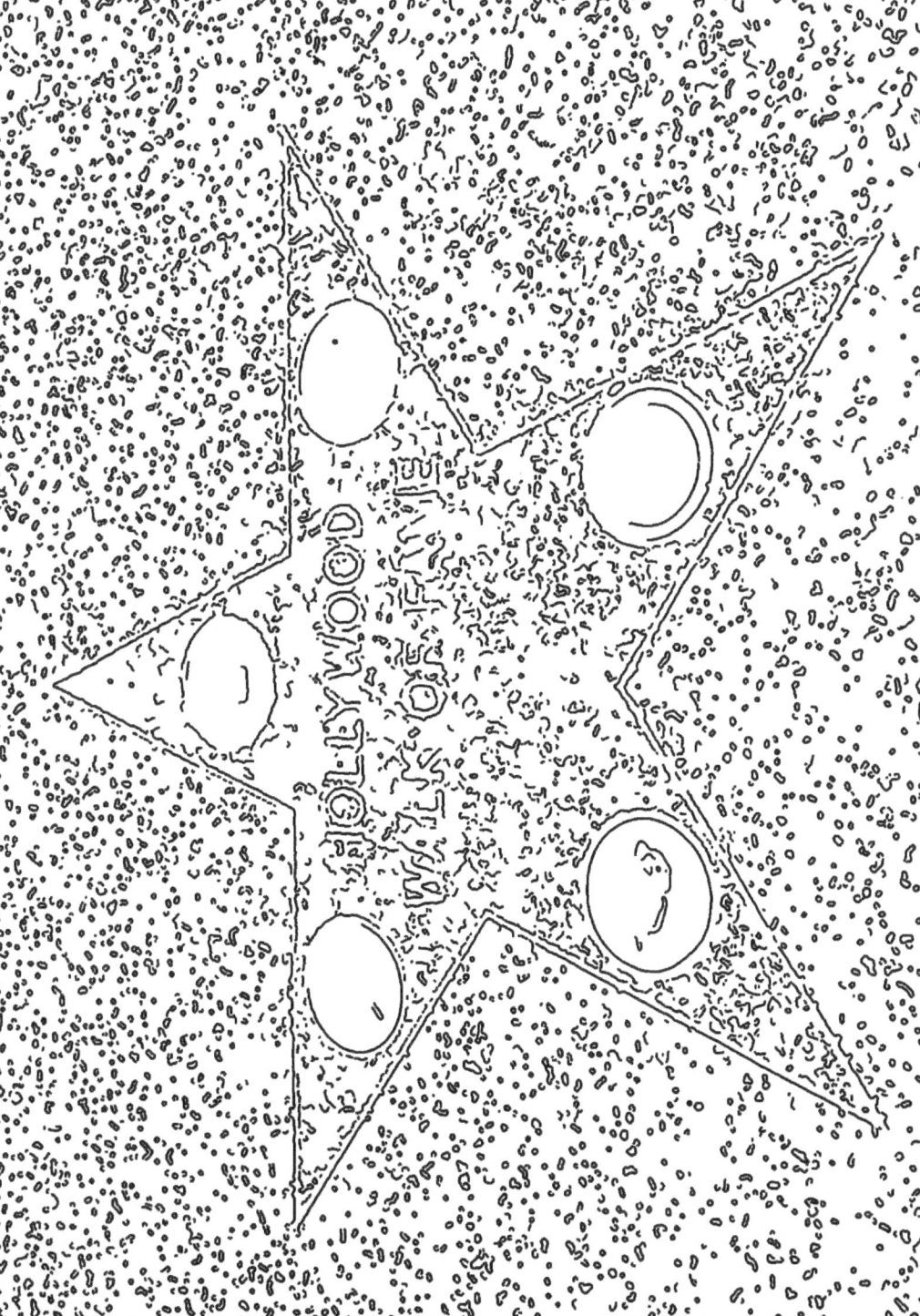

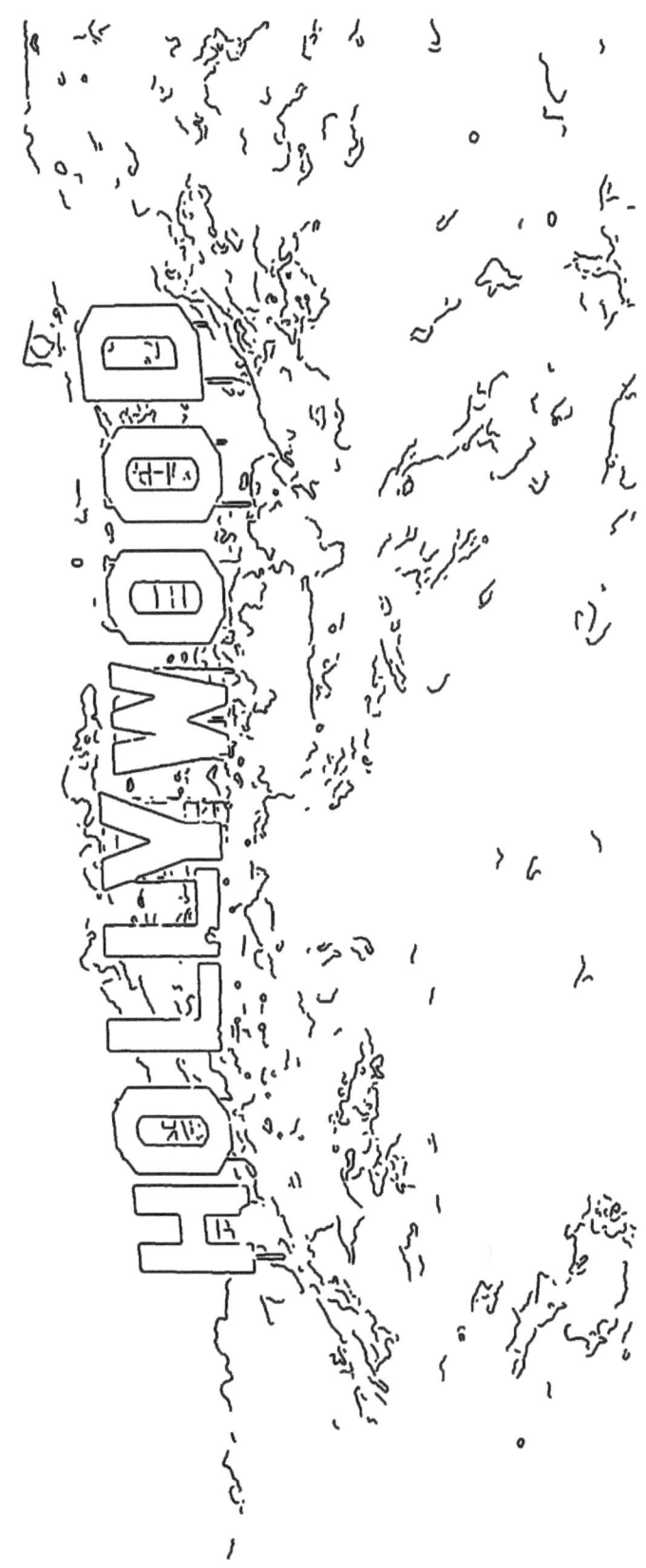

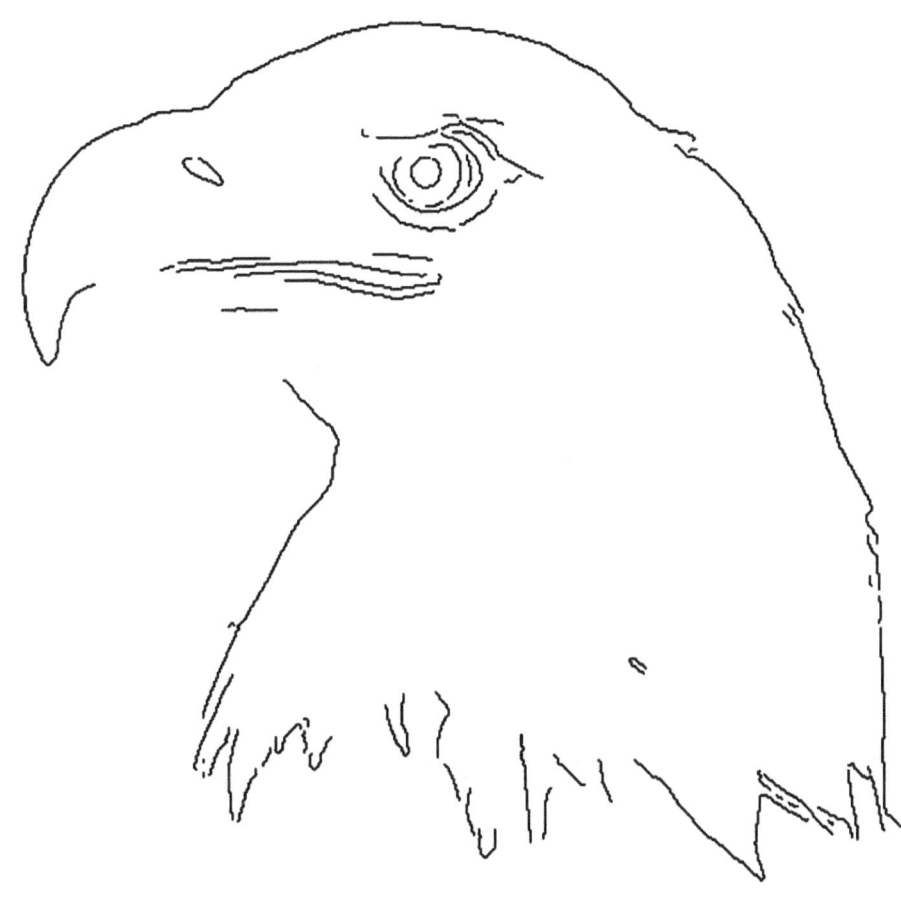

www.ingramcontent.com/pod-product-compliance
Lightning Source LLC
Chambersburg PA
CBHW080635190526
45169CB00009B/3399